5-Minute Classroom Management Hints

37 Proven Ways to Manage Your Classroom and Keep Your Sanity

Katrina Ayres

Books and eBooks by Katrina Ayres

*All The Ways I Screwed Up My First Year of Teaching
And How You Can Avoid Doing It, Too,* 2012

*Classroom Management Strategies That Work:
Strategy 1, Classroom Routines,* 2014

The Classroom Teacher's Coloring Book, 2015

*The Affirmations and Encouragement Coloring Book
For Grown-Ups,* 2015

ISBN: 152392862X
ISBN-13: 78-1523928620

CONTENTS

INTRODUCTION

LET'S FACE IT. Teaching is hard. Even if you love it and are really good at it, teaching takes a lot of energy. You have to think quickly on your feet, but also plan thoughtfully. You need to somehow respond correctly to all kinds of immature people (and children, too.) You have to organize a room full of tools, toys, and equipment. You have to find a way to help a bunch of other people (your students) stay organized, too. You are responsible for the safety, emotional well-being, and intellectual development of a roomful of rowdy and possibly hormone-infused kids. And, oh yeah, you need to entertain and inspire them. And stick with the schedule.

Some teachers make all of this look easy. They seem to just know the right thing to do in every situation. If you never worry about what's going to happen in your class each day, this isn't the right book for you. Just put it down now and back away slowly. (Or buy it for a friend.)

This book is a collection of short hints and tips about how to get along in the classroom. They first appeared in a series of emails called the *Monday Morning Sanity Boost* that I send each week to educators like you. Some of the hints you will agree with, and some of them you won't. Some will seem too easy to work, and some you will already be doing. All of them are things I've learned through my own teaching experience and a whole lot of mistake-making. I hope you find some ideas that will make your experience in the classroom a little easier and more fun so you can become the inspiring educator you always knew you were meant to be.

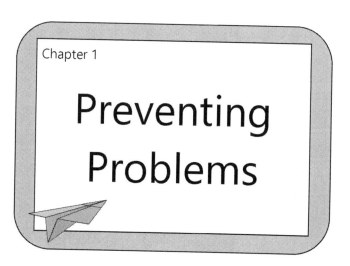

Chapter 1

Preventing Problems

T HE EASIEST PROBLEMS to solve are the ones that never arise, and preventing problems is much easier than fixing them after they happen.

This chapter covers a wide range of topics, from how to develop "withitness" to spending less time grading papers to taking your class outside to "selling" your classroom routines to your students. What they all have in common is the theme of solving problems before they start.

A few of these ideas will require a little preparation and thinking ahead, but if you can master them you will save yourself hours of time and an amazing amount of emotional energy.

WHAT GREAT TEACHERS DO AUTOMATICALLY

HAVE YOU EVER noticed that truly great teachers – master teachers – often appear to possess some sort of extra Spidey sense? They manage to be exactly where they need to be at exactly the right time to collect the paper airplane before it takes flight, separate the arguing students before they start punching each other, and catch the tub of paint before it hits the floor.

The uncanny thing is, they can do this while they are running a reading group, giving a demonstration, or helping students with their work, even with their backs turned! In fact, most of the time they don't even appear to know they are doing it.

This talent, called "withitness" is achieved through the practice of "monitoring and adjusting," two phrases we all learned in back in teacher college. In theory it's easy to understand. You check out what's going on (monitor) and you change what you're doing to make it better (adjust.)

In practice, it's not that easy. Of the thousands of things going on in a classroom at any moment, how do you know what to pay attention to, when to intervene, and exactly what to do? If you ask a master teacher this question, they usually say something like, "It's just experience." It's not that they don't want to be helpful, it's just become so automatic they do it instinctively.

If you need to develop withitness, I suggest you monitor three things: the quality of the energy or buzz in the room, the posture and gaze of key students, and anything that is moving.

Energy and buzz are created by what the students are paying attention to and/or talking about. If you notice a sudden change in noise level or tone, figure out where it's coming from and get there either verbally or physically as soon as you can. You don't need your eyes for this, which is why master teachers seem to have eyes in the back of their heads.

Secondly, you will quickly learn which students can influence the mood of a class. Popular students, students who tend to act out for attention, and so-called queen bees or bullies are all good to monitor. Look at their hands. Are they under the desk? Look at their eyes. Are they sending messages across the room? Do they appear to be concealing something by hunching over or turning sideways? Again, get there as soon as possible and try to figure out what's going on.

Finally, pay attention to anything that is moving. A student getting up, something rolling across the floor, feet, hands, objects getting ready to fall – it could be anything. Motion means change. Most change is fine, but some you will need to influence by moving the object, redirecting a student, and so on. Look for patterns, especially if something disruptive seems to happen whenever you detect this type of moving object or student. When you see it start to happen, do what you can to prevent it.

THE POWER OF THE DOOR

IF YOU COULD take just one action that would create a positive environment in your classroom and cut misbehaviors in half, would you do it? How about if it didn't involve any money and took about 10 seconds per student?

Every master teacher I know takes this action, yet many teachers dismiss it as unimportant. What is it? Stand at the door as your students enter the classroom. I know! It's almost too simple, right? Just standing there will help, but if you want to experience the real power of the door, make sure you also do these three things while you're there:

1) Greet your students by name. This will help the student feel like a person, not just one of the crowd that the computer assigned to your room. Engage in a quick, personal conversation, too, like asking how the game went last night, or giving them a compliment. Smile.

2) Give a quick, polite, specific direction about what they should do next, such as, "Please go to your seat and silently work on this assignment." Smile.

3) Scan the room as students are getting settled, and recognize on-task behavior. Your recognition will be more effective and powerful if it is given to the group instead of calling out specific students. It should also be specific, such as "I see that most people went to their seats right away and are working silently. Good job." Smile.

I know it seems simple, but I promise you will notice a

difference if you meet your students at the door consistently.

SHOULD STUDENTS SIT WHERE THEY WANT EACH DAY?

No, STUDENTS SHOULD not sit where they want each day. End of story. Have a nice day.

Haha! Just kidding. I can actually think of two good reasons for students to choose where they sit:

1) As a reward or incentive.
2) So the teacher can learn which students are dysfunctional when they sit together and separate them when making a seating chart.

On the other hand, there are many reasons to assign seats. A few of the reasons are about making things easier for the teacher, but most make it better for the students in some way. Here they are, in no particular order.

1) **Reduces anxiety for students**. Most people like to know what to expect. Your students are no different. When they don't know where they are going to sit, they can feel insecure.

2) **Cuts down on bullying opportunities.** Some students intimidate other students to get preferred seating. Having a seating chart makes this less likely to happen.

3) **Gives reluctant learners a better chance to succeed.** When given a choice, the more eager students are likely to sit up front and the students who struggle will sit in back. The students who struggle will then struggle even more.

4) **It's real world practice for your students**. In the real world, you don't always get to sit by who you want (particularly on airplanes) and your students

need to learn how to cope.

5) **Allows for differentiation for special needs,** including ADD/distraction, left-handed vs right-handed, vision impairments, hearing impairments, movement needs (such as standing at their seat or walking around.)

6) **Saves steps for the teacher.** Putting students who need extra help near the teacher saves steps and allows the student to get help faster.

7) **It is more fair** than letting dominant students get the best seats.

8) **Helps the teacher learn students' names,** which helps the teacher develop positive relationships with students.

9) **Helps a sub learn students' names** (assuming the students actually sit in their seats.)

10) **Makes attendance easier.** No need to call out names or ask students to report who is absent. Just look for empty seats.

11) **Can facilitate efficient paper passing.** If you can create a seating chart that is aligned with your grade book, it can save you hours.

12) **Can help students make new friends.** I discovered one of my best friends in high school when we were assigned seats next to each other.

13) **Tardy students don't have to disrupt class to find a seat.** They already know where they belong.

14) **Allows the teacher to make sure desks and chairs are the appropriate size.** Have you ever sat in a too-small chair or tried to write on a too-tall table? You can make needed adjustments when the student uses the same chair each day.

Make things better for your students and for yourself. Assign seats.

THE DOWNSIDE OF FEWER DISCIPLINE PROBLEMS

WHEN MY CLASS was out of control, I didn't get much work out of my students. I wasted so much time on power struggles, warnings, arguments, and waiting for the class to be quiet that there wasn't much time left for class work.

Once I got my class under control, I started to have another problem – how to keep up with all the work my students were turning in! Maybe you've been there, too – you give your students a few assignments, and suddenly you have a huge pile of papers to sort, grade, and record. It looks like hours and hours worth of work, and your weekend is looking like another boring round of sitting on the couch, watching TV and trying to get through it all.

One way to cut through the clutter and possibly reclaim at least some or your weekend from the Paper Mountain of Doom is to have your students work in spiral notebooks or lab books.

For elementary classrooms I recommend a different color notebook for each subject, say one for writing, one for math, and one for science or social studies. For secondary you can have one color of notebook for each period of the day. That way you can tell at a glance what the notebooks are and you don't have to spend lots of time sorting all that paperwork out. I also recommend teaching the students to put their name and the date on each assignment so you don't have to flip to the front of the notebook to see whose work it is.

Kids can copy assignments off the document camera or board, or out of workbooks. If the students are too young to do that, or if you need worksheets with lots of detail that would take forever to copy, the students can use glue sticks (not white glue, for obvious reasons) to glue the worksheets into the spiral binders.

When you want to check work for completeness (but not for correctness) have the students open their spirals or lab books to the correct page and lay them flat on their desks. You can do this for homework at the beginning of the day, or at the end of the period as a dismissal procedure. The teacher, an instructional assistant, a parent volunteer, or student volunteer can go around and check for completeness while the students are occupied with the next activity, such as a reading assignment, small group discussion, or lab.

To check work for correctness, collect the notebooks from a quarter of your students every day, Monday through Thursday. Have the students stack the notebooks in a pile on your desk, open to the first unchecked assignment. Then between classes, or when you have five minutes here or there, check one, make corrections to it, and close it up. You'll be surprised how many notebooks you can get done if you don't have to get them out and put them away every time you want to work on them.

BECAUSE I SAID SO

I PERSONALLY LOVE it when a principal says "Because I said so" when I ask why I have to do some seemingly illogical task, such as wrapping my bookcase in paper at the end of the year. "Because I said so" makes it SO much more likely I will happily follow the directions. (I hope you hear the sarcasm dripping from every word I am saying.)

Yet… I have been known to occasionally utter those dreaded words myself. Sometimes I'm just tired of constantly explaining myself and justifying my decisions to someone who has only been on the planet a fraction of the time I have. (And sometimes I'm just tired.)

You can inoculate yourself against the temptation to say "because I said so" by creating a student-centered rationale for your classroom routines, procedures, and rules. The important words here are "student-centered." The question to ask yourself is: How will it benefit the students to do whatever it is I am asking them to do? The more you can tune in to what the students want, the more likely they will want to do what you ask.

Consider these examples:

Task	Bad Reason	Teacher Centered	Student Centered
Put your name on your paper	Because I said so	I'm tired of figuring out who turned in what	You want to get credit for all your hard work
Line up quietly	Because I said so	You're giving me a headache with all your noise	When we are ready, we can go to lunch

You do not have to explain yourself every time you ask the students to do something. But it's a good idea when you are first teaching them a classroom routine, and it's also a much, much better reply when challenged than "Because I said so."

WANT TO HOLD CLASS OUTSIDE?

THE SUN WAS shining (a rarity here in Western Oregon) and the students in my most well-behaved class were restless. To tell the truth, so was I. We were all dying to get outside, and there was a safe, grassy courtyard right outside our door. So I figured, "Why fight it? They're a responsible bunch. They just have a touch of Spring Fever. They deserve a little change of scene."

I decided a reading assignment would be just the thing. I quickly gave them a few guidelines, and out we went.

Well, it was a total disaster. Rolling students, wandering students, whining students, grass fights, stick fights, imaginary spider attacks... you name it, we had it.

I herded them all back inside and spent the rest of the period trying to get them to settle down. The "good" students were mad at the students who had ruined it for everyone, and the misbehaving students were mad at me for making them the bad guys. Everyone suddenly needed a drink of water. Several students remembered items they had left outside. What I had intended as a refreshing change of scene had turned into a negative experience for all of us.

Actually, I could have taken those students outside successfully. The problem wasn't the students, it was me. I hadn't set them up for success. With only a few brief words of instruction, I expected them to somehow know exactly how to act in a completely different environment than the one they were used to.

Try to avoid holding class outside (or anyplace different than usual) until you have explicitly taught (not just told) your students how to be successful in that environment. Make a list of everything you can think of that could go wrong, including forgotten materials, students who don't like sitting on the ground, creepy crawlies and other likely distractions, and so on. Imagine how your "ideal student" would handle each of those issues and thoroughly demonstrate and teach those procedures to your entire class. Have a dress rehearsal inside where they all practice what to do.

The next step is to try the new environment for a few minutes to see how it goes. Let the students know you'll be testing it out for 10 minutes, and that you'll stay out longer next time if all goes well. Be sure to bring them back inside while they are still experiencing success. Recognize and celebrate what went well so the students will know exactly what they did right.

Holding class in a new location can be a challenge, but it can also be a relationship-building treat for you and your students. Plan and teach for success, and enjoy the change of pace.

ATTENTION-GETTING MISBEHAVIOR

I HAD JUST about had it with one of my third graders. All day long it had been one thing after another. Shouting out, clowning around, throwing things, making faces and fart noises, wandering the room... you name it, this student was doing it.

I finally just about lost it when he walked up to me while I was addressing the class and interrupted me mid-sentence to show me his new watch. Couldn't he see I was busy? And then I finally realized he was acting out to get attention.

Common wisdom says the way to "extinguish" attention-getting behavior is to ignore it. In my experience this doesn't really work. I find what usually happens is the attention-getting misbehavior will keep accelerating until you finally snap and react in some way. Once the misbehaving student gets a reaction, the misbehavior is reinforced, making it more likely to happen again.

One way to break this cycle is to give students the attention they are looking for before their misbehavior starts. I call it preventative attention.

If you have students who tend to act out to get attention, shower them with attention the moment they arrive in your room, before they've had a chance to start misbehaving. Say hello when they walk in. Ask their opinion about something (anything!) Ask them to show another student how to do something. Notice and comment on something they are doing right. Do not be fake and weird about it, but keep it going as consistently as you can for as long as you can.

If your students are already acting out, do what you need to do to stop the misbehavior, then start the positive attention routine as soon as possible. For example, when the third grader tried to show me his watch during direct instruction, I smiled and said, "Show me during recess, honey," and gestured toward his desk for him to sit down. Then I quickly called on him to answer a question I knew he could answer.

It may seem like this takes a lot of time and energy, and it does. But it takes even more time and energy to deal with all that attention-getting misbehavior all day long while trying to stay positive and maintain your sanity.

Do yourself a favor and give your needy students a little preventative attention. It couldn't hurt, right?

PRACTICE MAKES PERMANENT

THINGS YOU WILL never hear a teacher say:
"Please write your spelling words ten times incorrectly."

"Look away from the ball."

"Place your fingers on the wrong keys, and practice your scales."

It makes absolutely no sense to ask a student to practice doing a skill incorrectly. In fact, when it comes to fundamental skills for academic success, we continually model best practices and give students many opportunities to practice getting it right, helping them develop the good habits we know will lead to success. Once they know how to hold their pencils, their creative ideas can blossom in writing and drawing. Once they know how to hold a book, they can read for hours without strain. It's all about how to use your tools correctly, and they way to do that is practice until you get it right.

So why in the world do teachers fail to ask their students to practice the correct way to perform basic behavioral skills, such as how to ask a question in class, how and when to sharpen their pencils, how to treat a textbook, how to use their phone or tablet for academics, and so on? Aren't they the same?

I have even seen teachers ask students to do behavioral skills incorrectly ("Who can show me the wrong way to sit in your seat?") in an effort to help them discriminate between the correct and the incorrect way. While I believe it is important for the teacher to show common mistakes and why they won't work (both in academics and behavior) asking students to practice doing it wrong will result in confusion, and ultimately, in the student developing bad behavioral habits that will get in the way of their academic learning.

You would never ask a student to demonstrate how to solve for X incorrectly on the document camera! Don't do it with behavior, either. Practice doesn't make perfect. Practice makes permanent. So teach your students the skills to help them succeed, and have them practice doing it perfectly so that they can succeed.

Chapter 2

How To Say It So They Will Do It

WHEN IT COMES to working with kids, what you say can be just as important as how you say it. One word can determine whether your students will gladly follow your leadership, or dig in and resist.

Adults are used to figurative language and rhetorical questions that can confuse younger people with less experience. Phrasing that seems polite to adults can be offensive to students.

This chapter explores a few simple ways to fix communication breakdowns, and a couple of ways to show your students how they can get what *they* want when they do what you ask.

WITHOUT TALKING! IS THAT CLEAR?

YOU MAY HAVE noticed that, upon occasion, students do not do things exactly the way you want them to. Just the other day I asked a class of elementary students to work on an assignment without talking. Not even one second later, more than half the class started chattering with each other.

The heat moved up my neck and into my head. My ears started ringing. I was furious. Not even a pretense at doing what I asked! The disrespect! I was about ready to let them have it.

But then I took a deep breath, a practice I recommend frequently, and asked myself two questions.

1) Would yelling, blaming, or punishing make the situation better or worse? (Answer: There is no situation that will be made better by yelling, blaming, or punishing.)

2) Had I ever explicitly taught these students *my* definition of *without talking*? I knew what I meant, but did the students? (I know. With. Out. Talking. How can you get *that* wrong? But stay with me...)

Since the answer to Question 2 was I had not explicitly defined *without talking*, it was possible they didn't know what I meant. I decided to give them the benefit of the doubt and teach them.

I got their attention and then in a very quiet, calm, non-sarcastic voice I said, "I'm sorry. I guess I never actually taught you what I mean when I say *without talking*. *Without talking* to me means your lips are completely closed and your throat is not making any sounds." Then I showed them what *no talking* sounded like and a few anti-examples, such as talking loudly, murmuring, quietly asking to borrow a pencil, and whispering. When I repeated my request for them to work without talking the room was silent.

Why did this work? I think there are two possibilities. Either they really didn't know what I meant (for instance, they thought it was okay to talk as long as they were talking about the assignment) or they didn't think I was going to enforce it. By stopping the lesson and making my expectations clear, I took away any excuses and let them know I meant what I said.

At times, talking to a young person is like having a conversation in a foreign language. The expectations you bring to the conversation may be different than theirs, and even the words you use may have different meanings. Before blaming the students, try teaching a lesson instead. After all, you *are* a teacher!

THE PROBLEM WITH QUESTION WORDS

HOW WOULD YOU feel if I did this to you? I offer you some food you don't really want. Maybe you aren't hungry. Maybe you don't like that kind of food. Whatever the reason, you politely say, "No thanks." Then I get angry with you for refusing and force you to eat it.

Sounds rude doesn't it? Even abusive. We would never do that to our students! But many adults make a simple word choice that sounds exactly like this to young people. It's when you ask a question when the student really doesn't have a choice.

To an adult, "Would you like to get to work now?" may sound exactly the same as "Please get to work now." The adult may even think the first phrase is more polite. For a young person the difference is huge. Asking a question when you don't mean it is not polite, it's beyond rude. It's deceitful to offer a choice if you don't really mean it, and kids don't trust people who deceive them. Older students who know what you mean are still annoyed by questions that aren't really questions and choices that aren't really there. They often express their annoyance by taking the question literally and answering, "No, I wouldn't like to get to work now, and I won't."

A good rule of thumb is don't use a question word if there's really no choice. Just make the request politely using please and thank you.

Why don't you give it a try? Wait! I mean... please give it a try!

WHEN TEACHERS USE THE S-WORD

D O YOU EVER use the S-word with your students? I mean *should* of course. When you *should* on your students, you may be confusing them, setting yourself up for a power struggle, and sounding negative. Here are three difficulties with the word *should*:

1) ***Should* can be confusing.** Consider this scenario:

Teacher: You should listen while I'm talking.

Student (thinking): I guess that's a suggestion. The teacher is giving me some advice. But I want to keep talking, and I think this conversation I'm having with my friend is really important, so I'm going to decide to keep talking. (Keeps talking.)

Teacher: I told you to stop talking!

Student: No you didn't.

I think you can see this will end badly. Young children are literal, and in this situation the child was literally right. The teacher did not actually say to stop talking. Older students will know what you mean, but might decide to game the situation and use it as an excuse not to follow your instructions. You will get better results with "It's time to listen now."

2) ***Should* may sound like scolding.**

Possibly because scolders often say, "You should know better," the word *should* can trigger shame. "You should put that book away" can sound like "You idiot! Why didn't you put that book away yet?"

Again, just use a polite, simple request such as "Please put your book away. Thank you."

3) ***Should* can cause resistance.**

23

How do you feel when someone tells you what you should do? For instance, "You should exercise" makes me want to burrow into the couch and eat a fudge sundae. It has the same effect on our students, too.

If you notice the S-word sneaking out of your mouth, try to replace it with the word *please*. Your students will be more likely to do what you ask, and you'll feel better about yourself, too.

WHO WANTS TO BE FIRST?

ONE OF MY favorite prompts is, "Let's see who can be the first to…" (as in "Let's see who can be the first to get out your book without talking.") After giving the prompt, I immediately recognize the students who are following the prompt by simply saying, "Your book is out, and so is yours. Thank you."

Everybody wants to be first. I don't care if you're four years old or forty years old. If you don't believe me, try standing in front of someone who's waiting in line at the grocery store, or watch people crowding the door at a play or concert. People even pay extra money to be the first to board a plane, even though they already have assigned seats. Don't they realize everyone will have to board before the plane can take off?

There are many ways to modify this prompt. For example, "I wonder which table group will be the first to put away all their materials?" might also come with a reward – getting to be the first table group to be dismissed, for instance. (Notice how I cleverly used the desire to be first twice!)

Another desire of every human being is to be "in the know." Otherwise, gossip mags would soon be out of business. We especially want to know what we are supposed to do (even if we might choose not to do it.) I use this desire in the classroom when I am trying to give directions and the students aren't listening very well.

When this happens to me, I stop trying to give directions, and instead look for a student (any student!) who is paying attention. I look at that student and say,

"You're going to know what to do, because you're giving me eye contact." Then I find another student who is paying attention and say, "You're going to know what to do because you're not talking." I keep doing until it gets quiet enough for the class to hear me and then recognize that most people are with me, and I'm just waiting for a few more.

When you try this it's best not to use the students' names because it may be embarrassing for the student you are trying to recognize. It may also seem like you are favoring that student. Just look at the student and address them in the second person (using "you.")

Give it a try and let me know how it works for you!

THE MAGIC WORD

I'M SUBBING IN a second grade class. It's 8:00 am and there is an assembly at 8:10. In less than 10 minutes, I need to establish my authority, take attendance, line the class up, and get them to the assembly. I am well aware the principal and all the other staff will be at the assembly, so I don't want my class to tumble into the assembly looking like an out-of-control pack of wild cats with me tagging along, looking frazzled and stressed.

So what do I do? I use the Magic Word.

The Magic Word is not *please* or *thank you*. Believe it or not, the Magic Word is… (wait for it…) *without*.

Without is a way of quickly setting limits when you don't have time to teach routines. With the second graders I said, "Please line up *without* running, and walk through the hallway *without* talking and *without* touching anyone."

This may sound negative, but in fact it gives the students a clear idea of what you want, and you will spend less time correcting them later. "Please walk to your place in line" works fine, but the student may not hear or pay attention to the crucial word, which is *walk*. When you add *without running*, you emphasize how you want the action done with one simple straightforward sentence.

Next time you don't have time to teach a routine or procedure the correct way (using the direct instruction model) try the shortcut word *without*. You may be surprised at how well it works.

SAY NEXT INSTEAD OF BUT

HAVE YOU EVER had one of those backhanded compliments? Like, "Wow! You actually smell good today!" Yeah, me too. And yet, too many times I see educators giving backhanded compliments to their students without even realizing it.

"You did a great job on that writing assignment, but you need to work more on your spelling."

"You got 99% of those questions right, but you need to do the last one over."

"You got ready for dismissal quickly, but you are still too noisy."

Do you notice what each of those sentences has in common? It's that nasty little word "but." My fifth grade teacher taught me that whenever someone uses a sentence with the word "but" in it, you can ignore whatever came before the "but" and just pay attention to the rest of the sentence, because that's what the speaker really means. And in truth, that's exactly what happens with our students. Many times, they give much more weight to the criticism than they do to the praise.

As educators we make statements like these because we want to soften bad news or criticism, or we want to let our students know how they can continue to make progress. Unfortunately, using sentences containing "but" don't do what we want, and may actually feel manipulative and dishonest to our students, which will cause them to resist us.

So what can we do instead? I suggest a simple word substitution. Any time you want to use the word "but," substitute "next."

"You did a great job on that writing assignment. Next, let's work on some of those spelling words."

"You got 99% of those questions right. Great job! Next, I'd like you to work on that last one again, and see if you can get it right, too."

"You got ready for dismissal quickly. Thank you. Next, I'd like you to wait quietly."

Words are important, and sometimes small changes make a big difference. Give it a try and let me know how it goes.

Chapter 3

Supporting Positive Behavior

L IKE IT OR not, students adjust their behavior based on how we treat them, which means we are partially responsible for their behavior. Teaching our students how to be successful students (and successful people) is one of the most important things we can do. It's also a delicate balancing act. Praise can backfire, and so can punishment.

The next section explores how to reinforce our students' positive behavior without embarrassing them or sending the wrong message, and how to correct negative behavior without appearing critical. Once again, subtle changes in wording can make a huge difference.

DON'T EMBARRASS YOUR STUDENTS WITH PRAISE

I'M IN THIRD grade and all done with my work. In my class, we were supposed to read a book if we finished early, so my nose is buried in a book and I'm off in another land. Suddenly my teacher says, "Katrina, thank you for reading." I feel confused and uncomfortable. I like hearing a kind word from my teacher, but my classmates are all glaring at me.

Public praise can be embarrassing for students and may also be perceived as manipulative. Yet we know our students need as much positive attention as we can give them. How can we express our appreciation for positive behavior without it backfiring?

Try these two simple hints. First, if you want to recognize individual students for their positive behavior, acknowledge them privately instead of publicly. Drop by their desk and quietly thank them for making the right choice. You could even write a note or give them a token, especially if tokens are part of your school's positive behavior support system.

On the other hand, if you want to acknowledge students who are doing the right thing publicly and encourage the rest of the class at the same time, don't use names.

Glance around and make eye contact with your model students, smile, and say, "Thank you to the early finishers who are following directions and reading. I appreciate it." Then follow the acknowledgement with a "next" statement requesting the rest of the class to do the same. This strategy allows you to publicly acknowledge students who are making a good choice while saving them from the embarrassment of being singled out.

WHY NOT TO SAY "I LIKE"

MOST OF US want to be more positive with our students. We know how damaging a constant stream of negative comments and barked orders can be. So we make a supreme effort to say complimentary things.

"I like the way Martha got started right away," we say instead of what we are thinking, which is, "Would you people sit down, shut up, and get started on your assignment already?" (Okay, maybe you never think anything like that. I admit it. Sometimes I do.)

It's a great idea to point out positive action as a subtle reminder of your expectations, and it's also a great idea to recognize and acknowledge what's going right. I even wrote a previous hint about it.

The problem is the phrase "I like," especially when it is linked to a specific student. When you say, "I like the way Martha got started right away," your students will hear, "I like Martha." And they already know you like Martha. Why wouldn't you? Martha always does what you want.

Younger kids will feel jealous. Older students understand you are talking about the action Martha is doing, but they are much less concerned with pleasing the teacher. Sometimes you will even hear them mutter, "Why should I care what you like, Teacher?"

A better way to publicly recognize positive behavior is to focus on the behavior instead of the student. Leave out "I like" and the student's name and go straight to the behavior. Look at the student or point to the student and say, "You started working right away. Thank you."

Everyone who hears will keep listening because the sentence started with "you." The student(s) who are being acknowledged will get the message you see and appreciate them, and the other students will have nothing to object to. You will look less like you are playing favorites, and more like you are objective and fair. It's a win for everyone!

So lose "I like" and watch your students respond to your positive praise.

THE MAGIC CONSEQUENCE

"I ONLY HAD to keep him in from recess once, and I never had a problem with him again."

"Once I called home, she became a perfect angel!"

"I've tried everything I can think of, and nothing works with that child."

Each of these statements expresses a belief that somewhere, somehow, there is a perfect consequence that will finally fix our students' problem behaviors. We just have to keep trying until we find out what that consequence is, and then all our problems will be over.

Of course, there's actually no punishment or reward that will work for every student, every time. For one thing, something that is a punishment for one student will be a reward for another. Not only that, but our students are savvy enough to use reverse psychology on us. "Mrs. Ayres, what do I have to do to get lunch detention? All my friends are there."

Luckily there is a magic consequence, but it's not a punishment or a reward. It's consistency. It's following through and keeping our promises. It's doing our best not to overreact one day and under-react the next. It means saying what we mean and meaning what we say.

Consistency doesn't mean we have to be inflexible or domineering, nor does it mean we have to be perfect. It also doesn't mean we have to keep on doing something that's not working. We can consistently offer choices to our students, consistently empower them to solve their own problems, and consistently apologize when we make our own mistakes. Consistency simply means that, regardless of our style, our students can rely on us.

Will this be easy? Will we be perfectly consistent all the time? Of course not. Consistency in teaching is at least as difficult as consistently hitting home runs. The only way to get better is to practice, make mistakes, make adjustments, and practice some more. Kind of like... learning!

THE SANDWICH APPROACH

"YOU NEVER EVEN notice me unless I'm doing something wrong!" yelled my favorite Attitude Girl middle school student as she slammed her book on the desk and stormed out of the room.

I was confused, hurt, and upset. From my point of view I was very patient with this student's frequent shout-outs, arguments, and direct challenges to my authority. All I had said was, "Please get to work."

Of course, I had redirected her several times during class, and come to think of it, all my interactions with her had been redirection. So maybe on some level she had a point. I was trying to help her succeed, both academically and behaviorally, but she perceived only criticism.

So what's the solution? Never redirect? Never coach students academically or behaviorally? Ignore behaviors until they become intolerable? Of course not! Part of our job as educators is teaching students the behaviors they will need to succeed in school and life.

If you find yourself in a similar situation, you may want to try the Sandwich Approach. Before correcting the student, take a moment to notice what the student is doing right, and mention that before giving a prompt. Follow the prompt with a positive "thank you." (Sandwich the correction between two or more positive interactions.)

For example, even though Attitude Girl wasn't working, she was already doing many things right. She was in the room, she was sitting down, she was keeping her hands to herself, she had her book out, her phone was stowed in her backpack… Actually, there were a huge number of positive behaviors she was exhibiting. All I needed to do was choose one or two of those positive things and say in a businesslike, non-emotional tone, "Jasmine, I notice you are already in your seat and have your book out. Next, I would like you to turn to page 26 and read the first question. Thank you." (Smile.)

Noticing what students are doing right is a powerful way to let them know you see them all the time, not just when they are acting out.

FLIPPED PRAISE

"GOOD JOB! NICE work! That's terrific!" While most students would probably rather hear phrases like these than constant injunctions to sit down and be quiet, many still find them annoying. This is especially true if the teacher is a nonstop praise gusher to the extent that any recognition or praise becomes meaningless. Your students come equipped with a built-in insincerity monitor, especially older students. They can tell when they are being patronized or manipulated. Your students like to be recognized, but not embarrassed.

Another problem with these praise phrases is they are vague. Even when the teacher sounds sincere, students may not know why they are being praised, or even which student(s) are receiving recognition. "Good job heading your paper," is much better, but I still think it can be improved by using flipped praise.

Flipped praise starts with verbal recognition of the positive action of the student and then adds an optional praise phrase at the end. For example, you could say "You put your heading on your paper. Nice work!" Other students who hear will automatically check to see if they put the headings on their own papers. Then when they hear the praise phrase, they know it's for them, too. If they realize they forgot, they will get a reminder without any negative bossiness or correction.

Make sure your tone of voice is even and businesslike when you offer flipped praise. It should not sound like, "At least *you* put your name on your paper. Everyone else in the room who didn't is in trouble." It should also not sound like, "Oh my gosh! Putting your name on your paper is the most amazing thing I've ever seen!" Just businesslike and calm. You are noticing. You are giving credit. You are moving on.

Give it a try and let me know how it works.

Chapter 4

Small Things That Make Us Crazy

YOU MAY HAVE heard the saying, "I have just one nerve left, and you're getting on it" or the proverb about the straw that broke the camel's back.

Sometimes it's the little things that make you want to quit teaching all together, even though they sound like no big deal when you complain about them to your friends.

In this chapter I offer solutions for a few of my pet peeves - students who follow you around, the infamous "why do we have to do this" question, and being asked the same question over and over again. When I tackle the question of why your most difficult students are never absent, watch out! You may even find a little inspiration.

STUDENTS TRAILING YOU

THERE ARE MANY things to love about second graders: they are cute, they try hard, they are proud of their accomplishments, and they say the most awesome things sometimes. One thing that isn't so great about them is the way they follow you around when they need help.

This phenomenon is not limited to second graders, of course. Why does no one have a question about the assignment when you say, "Are there any questions?" but they all suddenly and urgently need your help the moment it is time to actually start working?

Possibly they don't want to admit they don't understand in front of the whole class. Possibly they want a little attention. Whatever the reason, individual help from their teacher is the only thing that will suffice, and of course they can't complete any work until they get it.

How you will handle this will depend upon the type of question your students are likely to ask, and whether or not you want to allow your students to talk while they work. For spelling questions, have the students attempt to spell the word on a sticky note and continue on with their writing. As you circulate through the room, quickly check the word, give a thumbs-up if it's right, or write it the correct way if it isn't. For math problems, they can write the problem number on the sticky note, and move on to the next problem while waiting for your help.

For procedural questions such as "What are we supposed to do?" instruct the students to ask each other. For information that can be looked up (such as a math or social studies fact) I teach them how to look it up and require they show me where they looked it up before asking me.

With second graders, I tell them I can't hear them when they come up to me. I can only hear them if they raise their hands. (Believe it or not, this sometimes works with middle school, too.)

.

WHY DO WE HAVE TO DO THIS?

Y OU'RE RIGHT IN the middle of direct instruction on a tricky new concept. You are busy explaining, demonstrating, and/or coaching students to help them understand. They are struggling. You are concentrating on how to explain so they will get it when someone blurts out, "Why do we have to do this, anyway?"

Without question, this is one of the most annoying things a teacher can hear. It seems to challenge the very essence of what we do as educators. It can interrupt the momentum of a lesson and even cause it to degenerate into an argument, especially if more students chime in, "Yeah, why *do* we have to do this?" As the cry echoes around the room, all hope of finishing your lesson flies out the window.

Luckily there are at least three effective ways to deal with this question: teach to it, dodge it, or bat it back.

Teach To It - Prevent the students from even asking The Annoying Question by giving them examples in your lesson introduction of why they will need to know the content or skill. Plan for it ahead of time so you will have several student-centered examples of why they will need this knowledge.

One great formula is, "Today we are going to learn [lesson topic.] There are many times you may need to know [lesson topic.] For example, if you are in [situation] you would need [lesson topic] to [be successful in the situation.]" Then ask the students to generate several more similar situations where they might need the content. The Teach To It approach is great because it can help your students be motivated to learn the content of your lesson and stick with it even if it is difficult for them.

Dodge It - The second way to deal with "why do we have to do this" is to dodge the question. I do this when I feel the students are asking the question for entertainment, diversion, or to challenge my authority. To dodge the question, calmly say "That's a great question! I'd be happy to discuss it with you after class." And then simply move on and keep teaching. This approach works because it denies the student the entertainment and drama of watching you get upset. It is also simple, direct, and quick.

Bat It Back - The third approach is to ask the class to come up with examples of when the skill or concept would be useful. You can ask them to pair share, write down examples, restate the rationale from the standards, or look for examples in their textbooks or workbooks. Hold each student accountable for doing some work to answer the excellent question of why they need to learn this skill. They may not be happy with the extra work, but they will be so much better informed... and will probably not ask again. This approach takes extra time, but can help your students learn to answer their own questions instead of depending upon the teacher.

DON'T REPEAT YOURSELF

IMAGINE YOU ARE on a game show. You have a chance to win thousands of dollars if you answer the question correctly. The host opens his mouth to read the question. What are you doing at that moment?

My guess is you are leaning forward with your eyes on the guy's face. You have your head turned slightly so your better ear is toward him. You are concentrating. You are focused. There is no way you are going to miss what he says next.

Scenario Two: Same game show, but this time you know the host will read the question three times and if you still didn't get it, you can ask him to repeat two or three more times. You may still be listening, but will you be giving the same level of attention? My guess is probably not.

The same is true for our students. When they hear us say the same thing over and over, they tend to tune out. For one thing, it's boring hearing the same thing over and over. For another thing, they know from experience exactly how many times you will say something before you really mean it.

I teach my students early on that I don't like to repeat myself. I tell them I understand they might not hear what I said the first time – that's totally normal. It's just that I get tired saying the same thing again. If a student asks me to repeat something I just said, I ask for another student volunteer to repeat it. "Oops, you must have missed it," I say. "Let's see who got it."

If you try this with your students, please, please avoid

sarcasm or a mean tone. Be businesslike and calm. Also, if none of the students can accurately repeat what you said, you may not have been clear and you will want to repeat it. And finally, please be sensitive to students with special needs and adapt as necessary.

If you make the decision that, for the most part, you will only say things once, you may be surprised how many of your students suddenly develop better listening skills.

WHY ISN'T THAT DIFFICULT STUDENT EVER ABSENT?

HAVE YOU EVER noticed that those students who are always acting up are almost never absent? They are there first thing in the morning, always hanging around in between classes, and won't leave after school! Why? Do they want to torture us?

Could it be you may be providing the only structure that student has? Could it be you are the only one who cares enough to set limits and say no every once in awhile?

In a funny, twisted kind of way those students are honoring you.

Take a moment to reflect on the value of what you do every day. Every day you are keeping students safe, leading by example, and showing them how a well-put-together adult behaves. Without even saying a word, you are teaching them that it is possible for an adult to be committed enough to show up every day.

They may not understand it now, but believe me, they are getting it deep down inside somewhere. It's possible they may realize it later. Or maybe not. But just take a moment right now to realize your incredible value in this world and accept my sincere thanks for doing your best to make this world a better place.

I honor you and your work. Please don't ever give up!

Chapter 5

Challenges To Our Authority

CHALLENGES TO YOUR authority will happen daily in the classroom. It's just part of the job.

Our students challenge us because it is a natural part of growing up. It's the way students learn the difference between right and wrong. It's the way they test out their own beliefs and learn to think independently.

That doesn't make it any less annoying, though. When you are trying to get everything accomplished, the last thing you need is someone testing your limits and refusing to follow directions.

In this section, I give a few hints about how to keep our students' natural need to challenge us from obstructing learning or damaging our relationship with them.

THE PROFANITY BUTTON

IT'S ALMOST NEVER a good idea to act upset or offended when a student uses profanity or any other type of inappropriate or emotionally charged language. It's an especially bad idea if there is an audience (such as the rest of the class.) Reacting with anger or shock will signal to the students that profanity is one of your buttons that they can push whenever they want to bring a little drama into the classroom. It may also embarrass students who accidentally say the word or don't know what it means.

But what to do instead? It depends on the situation and you will need to follow your school's policies and guidelines. Here are a few strategies to try.

1) **Teach and agree upon expectations as a class**. If you choose this approach, please do not get drawn into making a laundry list of inappropriate words or letting kids ask, "Is it okay to say ____?" Explain that words can encourage and build up and words can hurt, and in your class you will use positive language. Tell the students to ask you privately if they are unsure if a word is appropriate for the classroom.

2) **Use humor**. When I was teaching a middle school computer class, there were plenty of opportunities for swearing. One time a really nice student tried to open a project she had been working on for two weeks and found that it had disappeared. She let rip with some language I thought she might not even know, much less be able to use in such a

colorful way. "Well, it's not often you hear THAT phrase in the classroom," I said. Everybody in earshot laughed, she apologized, and it was over.

3) **Ignore it.** This is another strategy for accidental swearing, under-the-breath swearing, or momentary loss of control. Be careful what you ignore, though. You do not want to appear as if you don't know what's happening in your class. If the class asks, "Did you hear what he just said?" say, "Yes, I did, and I'll be talking to him later." Then keep teaching!

4) **Use it as a teachable moment.** Sometimes students are just repeating what they have heard at home or at the movies. This is an especially good strategy for racist, sexist, or homophobic language. You can start by saying, "You know, I've heard that phrase going around the school lately and I'm not sure people really understand what they are saying." Then you can go on to explain why the word may be offensive and is not appropriate for school. You can do this with the whole class or you can quietly pull the student aside.

5) **Act like you're thinking, take a deep breath, and wait about 10 seconds before responding.** In about 80 percent of the cases the student will back down. If not, you will have time to think about what to do next. In some cases, you still may not know what to do. If that happens, you may want to say something like, "Hmm. I'm going to need to think about how to handle what you just said. I'll let you know once I've decided."

No matter what the situation, your best response is going to be a calm one. An explosive or reactive response will almost always make the situation worse.

BE YOURSELF

A BUNCH OF us are eating lunch together in the staff room. The topic of discussion is the antics of a certain student. He's definitely having one of those days. As we "professionally" compare notes, it is clear that the student has disrupted every class so far - except one. He was fine in Mr. Garcia's class. In fact, Mr. Garcia never has any problem with him.

As we jokingly tease Mr. Garcia about his superpowers as a teacher, a strange idea dawns in my head. Mr. Garcia is a little nerdy. His room is filled with plants hanging from the ceiling, climbing from the walls, draped over the curtain rod… every possible place where a plant could be, there is one. And guess who is also into plants, and in fact comes in before school every day to help water Mr. Garcia's plants? You guessed it. That student.

So what am I saying? That every classroom should have a million plants in it? No, what I'm saying is let your students see and know what you're into. If you love a certain sports team, wear the colors on game day. If you sew medieval costumes, bring them in so the students can see them. Love shoes? Mountain biking? Poodles? Handmade pasta? Square dancing? Balloon animals? Whatever it is, share it! And don't get so focused on your long teaching to-do list that you forget to be yourself.

Even if your students think you're weird for liking whatever it is, it will make you more human to them. After, all the human connection is what teaching is all about. Plus - big bonus - students will challenge you less if they can relate to you as a person.

HOW TO GET MORE CONFIDENCE

Y OU DON'T HAVE to be a new teacher to feel insecure. All of us have felt the squishy nervous feeling in our stomachs that happens whenever you are in a situation you're not quite sure you can handle. Your armpits and hands dampen. Your mouth gets dry. Your heart pounds and you have trouble breathing. You may even get lightheaded or need to run to the bathroom.

Unfortunately kids are really good at detecting when we are feeling insecure and capitalizing on the situation to create drama and/or get out of work. You can try to fake confidence (breathing helps, as does deodorant) but wouldn't it be better to actually *have* confidence?

So what exactly is confidence, and where can you get it? One definition of confidence (from Dictionary.com) is "belief in oneself and one's powers or abilities." I think the best way to acquire a belief in your powers and abilities is to have a well-thought-out plan.

I have a friend who jumps out of airplanes. He isn't nervous about it at all because he knows exactly what to do in just about every situation that can come up. There are protocols for what to do if the weather is bad, if the parachute doesn't open, or if he starts to drift away from his target landing area. In other words, he has thought about what could go wrong and made a plan to either prevent it (pack your chute correctly) or correct it (have a backup chute.)

I recommend all new teachers (and experienced teachers, too) try to think of everything that can possibly go wrong in their classrooms. Then make a procedure that will prevent that thing from happening, and teach it to your students. If I'm worried that students will sharpen pencils while I'm talking, I teach them what to do if their pencil breaks. If I think they'll cheat on a test, I teach them how to arrange their desks. And so on.

Experienced teachers have a big advantage here, because they have had so many things go wrong already that they instinctively know what to plan for. But new teachers can do it, too. The problem is, many of them don't. I know I didn't. My idea of how to prepare for the classroom was to go to the teacher supply store and buy a bunch of thematic lesson plan books. What I should have done was think about the logistics of my classroom and write a bunch of lesson plans to use at the beginning of the school year.

I always say, "Confidence is natural when you know what to do." And thinking it through ahead of time will help you know what to do.

Do You Need Some Help?

I ADMIT IT. I am sometimes sarcastic with my students. Most of the time it's a bad idea, but every once in awhile it turns out all right.

One day I was teaching an eighth grade algebra class. As I scanned the room I saw two students laughing and joking together during a work period. My sarcasm demon appeared and I heard myself saying with "the tone," "Did you two need some help back there?"

To my surprise one of them looked at me respectfully, and humbly answered, "Yes, I do."

Well, then.

How many times I had yelled at, penalized, or been annoyed with a student who simply didn't know how to get started? True, students should ask for help, but I can't really blame them for not wanting to appear stupid or weak in front of their friends. What do *you* do when you don't know how to get started with something? Procrastinate, right? Talk to your friends, right?

Ever since that day I have tried to ask off-task students if they need help before jumping in with a reprimand. It's shocking how often they say yes.

Chapter 6

Managing Your Emotions

I ADMIT IT. There are times when I am angry, offended, and upset with my students. And while I try my best to respond appropriately, sometimes it is difficult. Really, really difficult.

No one expects you to be perfect, but you don't want to be the subject of a viral video, either. Here are a few hints on how to maintain your cool in the classroom.

WHISPER INSTEAD OF YELLING

IT WAS ONE of those days. I hadn't slept well. Everything went wrong while getting ready for work. Traffic was a mess. When I got to school I was already grumpy, and then it seemed my students had all had the same kind of morning. My most reasonable requests were met with resistance. Attitude was everywhere. I was about to snap.

Have you ever had a day like this? A day when nothing was going right and emotions were running high? And then *that* student says *that* thing, and you are *that* close to completely losing it?

Whew! I'm glad I'm not the only one!

You already know that when you are in a situation like this you will only make it worse if you lose your temper and yell. Losing your cool make you look, well, uncool. You will scare the younger kids and the older kids will laugh at you. No matter what, if you lose it, you will lose.

So take a deep breath and try this simple strategy.

Whisper.

If nothing else, whispering keeps whatever you are saying from echoing throughout the school. But it also helps dissipate the negative energy so you can keep your temper. When you hear yourself yell, you lose control. When you hear yourself whisper, you keep control.

Not only that, but your energy is contagious. When you yell, your students' energy will escalate to match. When you whisper, they will tend to quiet down.

So the next time you want to yell…whisper!

TAKE A BREAK

IT'S ONLY HALFWAY through Monday morning and you're already tired, stressed-out, and wishing for the weekend. Decisions that are normally a breeze are tough to make. Student behavior that normally doesn't bother you makes you mad, and your overreactions are causing your students to act up even more. You're klutzy and disorganized and your mind is like peanut butter.

In other words you've been working too hard!

For the sake of yourself and your students, it's time to take a break. Tonight make sure you get some sleep. Possibly even take a nap as soon as you get home. And make sure you schedule some time for fun in the next day or two. You deserve it and your students deserve a better-rested you.

But what about right now? How are you going to make it through the rest of the day?

I suggest taking several short breaks throughout the day to do something for yourself that is fun, nurturing, and energizing. Take the time right now to make a list of things you like to do and make it a point to do a few of those things today. Sometimes just making the list will make you feel better! Here are some ideas to get you started:

Dance, drink water, pop bubble wrap, drink coffee, go outside and look at the sky, doodle, yell whoo-hoo!, read a non-work related book, make funny faces in the mirror, stretch, rip or crumple paper, meditate, color, tell some-one a joke, read an inspiring quote, read a chapter from this book, sing nonsense words, go for a short walk, or eat chocolate.

As a teacher you spend most of your day nurturing others. Take some time for yourself from time to time, and watch your effectiveness increase.

****

A GIFT FOR YOU!

If you like to color to relieve stress, I have a gift for you! It's the PDF version of my coloring book for teachers called *The Classroom Teacher's Coloring Book*.

Please go to
PositiveTeachingStrategies.com/colorbookbonus
to claim your copy.

****

ARGUMENTS WITH STUDENTS

HAVE YOU EVER argued with your students? Me too. And if you are like me, even if the students comply with you, apologize, or admit they were wrong, you still feel like a loser because you might have damaged your relationship with your students.

It might be helpful to ask yourself why you want to argue in the first place. If your goal is to persuade the student to act or think differently, one of the worst things you can do is tell them they are wrong and force them to defend themselves. You can no longer influence the student because you are both busy trying to win and make the other person lose.

The best way to win an argument with a student is to stop trying to win. Instead focus on winning them over. Build rapport by listening and trying to honestly understand their point of view before trying to change their opinions. Ask them to explain more. Listen to what they say. Repeat it back to them. Try to empathize. Even if you don't agree, see if you can understand why they are feeling the way they do. You will have a much better chance of getting them to see your point of view if you have truly listened to theirs.

How Not to Lose Your Temper

Teachers are human, and humans get angry. When you're dealing with students, parents, and possibly administrators and colleagues who are experts at pushing your buttons, it's inevitable. Most of the time we can deal with it pretty well, but what about if you are not just angry, but furious and in danger of losing it entirely? What then?

I think we can all agree that yelling, throwing books, breaking things, punching walls, and getting physical with students will only lead to more problems. And of course you would never do any of that if you were calm.

The problem is, in this moment of rage you are not thinking rationally, if indeed you are thinking at all. Your head is buzzing, your vision has narrowed to a little pinprick, your teeth are clenched, and all you can hear is your pounding heart. This is a true emergency, and what you need is an emergency plan.

Emergency plans need to be put in place *before* there's an emergency. You think about what you can do to minimize damage and keep everyone safe. You have a backup plan and a way to get help, and you practice it ahead of time. Once you have a plan, you no longer have to make decisions during the emergency. You just follow the plan.

While creating your plan be sure to take into account how you will de-escalate yourself. Some common ways are breathing, drinking water, clasping your hands behind your back, and so on. Also think about how to escape the situation gracefully. I like to tell the student I can't talk right now and then go to my desk or step out into the hallway.

You might also find it helpful to have a trusted colleague you can call for help. That colleague can take the student away for a minute or two or take over your class while you go to the bathroom or go to the drinking fountain.

Even if things don't go perfectly you will have a much better chance of success if you have planned ahead. So go ahead, take a minute and think about what your best self would do in that situation. And just know that no one is perfect and everyone gets angry, even teachers.

DON'T PANIC

DON'T PANIC! I'M not promising you everything will be okay. How could I know that? The only thing I know for sure is panicking won't help. It will just take a bad situation and make it worse. How do I know this? Lots of panicking in the classroom.

Emotions are like lemmings. When you follow them you end up running yourself off a cliff. Sure, be scared. Sure, admit you don't know what to do. Hey, even tell yourself you're totally screwed. But don't panic.

I know the feeling, and it isn't pretty. One time I was standing in front of 42 seventh graders, many of whom swaggered into the room in gang-banger droopy pants and baseball hats (which was a violation of dress code.) They are talking trash to each other across the room and completely ignoring me, the teacher, standing in the front of the room on the first day of class.

Panic seems reasonable. However (I remind myself) not helpful. What will change if I take a moment to compose myself? Nothing. They will keep up the talking, but I will have regained my composure. Breathing a couple of times, I take a look around the room. Of the 42, only seven are actually trash talking and being loud. The others are either quiet or talking with their friends – just what I would do while waiting for class to start. True, I still have a problem, but it's not the all-encompassing rebellion I initially thought.

I decide to pretend the seven yahoos aren't there and address the 35 that are just fine (and waiting to see how I'm going to react.) Another deep breath, and I start class just as I had planned. No it wasn't perfect, and yes I did need to redirect. But at least I kept my sanity and didn't alienate the rest of the class by blaming them for the minority of students who were acting out.

Don't panic and you may live to see another day!

Chapter 7

Regaining Control Of The Class

NO MATTER HOW carefully you plan or how thoroughly you teach routines and expectations to your class, there will still be those days when chaos seems to reign.

Maybe something happened at lunch. Maybe something happened at home. Maybe the schedule is all messed up. For whatever reason, things are not going your way.

For those moments, it's important to have a few tricks in your back pocket that can help you regain the helm and get your students on track again.

I hope you won't need to use these techniques often, but when you do, here they are.

HONEYMOON PERIOD OVER?

YOU KNEW FROM the first day of school that a couple of your students were going to be a challenge, but the rest of the class seemed fairly easy to manage. On the whole they were pretty good at following directions and you were excited about all the fun activities you were going to be able to do with this group.

Then you started noticing some not-so-welcome changes. Less homework is turned in. The noise level is higher. There are more side conversations and off-task behavior. You have to redirect often and your tone is sometimes impatient and negative. It seems as if half the class (or more) is now acting like the challenging students from Day 1. It's like a disease spreading through your class. I call it Octoberitis.

If Octoberitis is infecting your class, it's time to re-establish your leadership immediately. There are many ways to do this, and one of the simplest is to rearrange your desks or tables. If your students are spending more time talking than working, maybe it's time to try a more traditional room arrangement where everyone is facing the teacher. Or maybe your students could benefit from a U-shaped arrangement that would allow you to see all your students and get to them quickly.

If students have been sitting in the same seating arrangement since the beginning of the year, they have developed micro-cultures throughout the room. Whatever is going on in these mini-nations is more important to your students than anything you are trying to teach them. It's time to break it up!

If you are a secondary teacher or your classroom uses tables instead of desks, rearranging your seating chart is easy. Number the tables or desks with stickers, labels, or post-it notes. Assign each student a number. Place the list of students and their numbers on the document camera, then meet them at the door as they arrive and ask them to find their new seats.

If you have individual desks your students may be able to move the desks themselves using a seating map. I have done this successfully with students as young as eight years old. (If you decide to do this, make sure you give explicit directions about how to avoid bumping into each other. It can also be helpful to challenge the students to make the move without talking.)

I recommend telling the students there will be a new seating arrangement before you make the change. Some students will need time to get used to the idea of sitting in a new place. When you are making the move, I also recommend an incentive (such as getting to listen to music during work time) if everyone makes it to their new seat quickly and quietly.

You may think this idea is too simple to work, but why not give it a try? You may be surprised how much of a difference it can make.

SPEED UP AND LOWER YOUR VOICE

D O YOU EVER feel like you're talking to yourself? I had this experience just last week. I was teaching a group of 29 adorable and very social fourth graders with the usual mix of students with ADD, Tourette's, spring hormones, and so on. All day it had been a struggle to hold their attention and I was working really hard to keep them on track without being negative.

After awhile I noticed my voice getting hoarse. Because I felt the students weren't paying attention, I had been talking loudly, rephrasing things, and repeating myself a lot. Suddenly I remembered the definition of insanity: continuing to do the same thing and expecting different results. I decided to do the opposite of what I had been doing. I lowered my voice and started talking faster.

Guess what? It worked! They leaned forward in their seats, quieted down, and became engaged with the activity. I have noticed students are often calmer and more attentive when I lower my voice but I had never tried talking faster at the same time.

Maybe our students are tired of hearing loud, bossy-sounding voices all day. Maybe their shorter attention spans like a quicker pace. For whatever reason it worked like a charm for me. Give it a try and let me know how it works for you.

WHEN CHAOS IS TAKING OVER

WHEN CHAOS SEEMS to be taking over it can be easy to lose your cool. Your heart rate soars, your armpits and palms dampen, your stomach clinches, and your self-talk goes into overdrive. "Yikes! My class is out of control! Nobody is working! They're so noisy! I'm a failure as a teacher! Help!"

It's very important in these situations to breathe. So do that first. Slowly. In then out. Next I suggest you look for anything and everything you can find that is going right.

It is highly unlikely that *everybody* is completely and totally out of control. Detach. Look around. Pretend you are a scientist observing your classroom through a one-way mirror. You are wearing a white lab coat and you have a clipboard. This white-coated, clipboard-toting observer's job is to look for anything and everything that is going right in the current moment and tell you about it. Your job is to recognize it and then tell your students about it.

For example, let's suppose that 80 percent of your students are off task. That's a problem, to be sure. However, it is also true that 20 percent of your students are on task. Look around. Notice who they are. Count them or estimate how many. Then recognize them, thank them, and make a request using the word "next."

Say something like this, in a super-calm-everything-is-totally-under-control voice: "I notice about seven people have started the assignment (are sitting in their seats, are looking at me, are not talking, are giving me their attention, etc.) Next I would like everyone to have a seat (look at me, look at me without talking, give me their attention, etc.)"

As more students comply, recognize that too. "Now half the class is working. Thank you. Now almost everyone is working. Great!" Once you get almost everyone going you can deal with whoever is left one at a time.

This works because it's a subtle form of peer pressure. Most of your students want to be normal. They want to be doing what everyone else is doing. If it seems everyone is out of their seats, they will be out of their seats. If most people are in their seats, they will want to be in their seats too.

It still surprises me how well this works. Give it a try, and see if it works for you!

Katrina Ayres

THREE WAYS TO QUIET A NOISY CLASS

I DON'T EVEN need to explain why you need today's hint. So when you need to quiet a noisy class that won't listen to you, here are three things you can try.

1) Turn on the document camera and put up a blank piece of paper. For older students write "Quiz," and tell the students to number their paper from 1-20 (even if you think they can't hear you.) Start writing the numbers while you think of some quiz questions. For younger students, tell them to copy you. You can start by drawing shapes, or writing numbers, or whatever they can do easily. Your "star" or "always" students will begin. Others will follow. And guess what? It's nearly impossible to write and talk at the same time.

2) Use a rhythm clap, echo, chant, or song. Ones that have "shhhhh" in them are good and ones that end with hands clasped are also good.

3) You may be able to use competition and peer pressure by giving a reward (such as group points, first to be dismissed, tokens, or preferential seating) to any group who is quiet within a time you set, and a bonus if the whole class makes it. You can count or use a timer. You can also give out first, second, and third place, with corresponding rewards. (Avoid giving out a prize only to the first group to quiet because then the other groups will have no more motivation to try.)

In general you will be most successful at quieting a

class if you remain quiet yourself and stay as positive as possible. Yelling, blowing whistles, and setting off alarms are some of the worst things you can do. They are entertaining and reinforcing and only add to the noise. No matter how you feel inside you need to remain outwardly calm as much as possible.

There are many ways to calm a noisy class. I would love to hear your favorites.

Chapter 8

Specific School Year Events

THE FINAL COLLECTION of hints in this book is about how to be ready for specific times of year, such as the first day of school and the last day of school. It also talks about some out-of-the-ordinary-yet-common events you will need to prepare for, such as getting a new student.

I truly wish someone had taught me what to expect and how to plan for these situations, because it took me several years to figure it out by trial and error. If you follow my advice (instead of doing what I did) you will have a much better time of it.

My First Day of School Disaster

FOR SOME REASON I used to think it was really important to take my students outside on the first day of school and teach them to "circle up." After we headed out to the field behind the school I made them hold hands and form a circle. Once they accomplished that (after a lot of nagging) we played a game.

Even though nothing horrible actually happened while we were doing this pointless exercise, I look back on it now as a disaster. Why? Three reasons:

1) I wasted 30-45 minutes on the first day of school teaching the students to do something we would rarely do in class. Every minute of the first day of school is precious and should be used to teach skills they will use every day, such as how to peacefully share materials. People remember best what they are first taught and what they learn when they are emotional. Harness the primacy effect and the emotion of the first day of school to teach students the skills they will need to succeed for the rest of the year.

2) The nagging and warning I mentioned. Our students need to learn to follow directions the first time.

3) The activity created false expectations about how fun my class would be. Imagine how exciting it was for my students to think we were going to go outside and play games a lot. Imagine how disappointing it was when reality set in the following week and they were expected to sit still

and listen. Disappointed people (my students) tend to attack whoever disappointed them (me.) It's okay to have fun on the first day of school (and every day of school) but try to have fun with your normal activities instead of creating false expectations.

Don't do what I did. Use that first day of school energy to teach your students the skills they will need all year long. You will thank me in May.

DON'T SMILE UNTIL THANKSGIVING

O F ALL THE horrible classroom management advice I have heard, "don't smile until Thanksgiving" has got to be just about the worst. The implication is if you act mean, strict, unsmiling, and cold, you will be able to intimidate your students into behaving. Then later (after Thanksgiving, presumably) you can lighten up and reveal you really aren't that bad after all.

There are probably a million reasons this is bad advice, but I know you are busy, so I will limit myself to three:

1) Today's students aren't easily intimidated. They either come from a home where adults (unfortunately) are much meaner than you could ever be, or a home where adults protect them from anything unpleasant (including mean teachers.) Most of today's students are not taught to submit to authority, no matter how unreasonable (and thank goodness for that.)

2) Consistency is the best way to teach your students appropriate behavior. There is no such thing as the giant consequence that will make everything all better. When you switch from mean to nice and back to mean again, your students will continue to misbehave, just to see where the line is today.

3) Building a positive relationship with your students has been shown time and time again to be one of the most effective ways to create respect. Students who respect their teachers are more likely to do what they ask. Students who feel their teachers hate them will resist and rebel.

My advice to you is smile a lot from the very first minute of school while you set logical, reasonable limits and build rapport with your students. They will be much nicer to you, I promise.

SPENDING WEEKS TEACHING ROUTINES

I REMEMBER THE first time someone told me I needed to spend two to four weeks (two to four *weeks!*) teaching my students how to do simple things like putting their names on their papers, bringing their notebooks to class, and closing the classroom door quietly.

I felt overwhelmed and panicky and my first thought was, "I don't have time for that! I have too much curriculum to cover!"

Can you relate?

Do you really need to spend weeks on classroom routines? The answer is yes.

Behavioral skills such as bringing materials to class, putting your name on your paper, asking for help, sharing space with other students, and so on, are foundational to academic learning. Behaviors that facilitate learning come first, then you can cover your curriculum effectively.

Jumping right into teaching your curriculum without thoroughly teaching classroom routines is the same as trying to teach essay-writing before your students know the alphabet – it's just going to be frustrating and counterproductive for everyone.

So take a deep breath, quell your panic, and commit to helping your students create positive learning habits that will serve them for a lifetime. The time you invest now will save you hours later on.

New Student Trick

A S A SAVVY educator you know the importance of reviewing rules, routines, and procedures frequently. Your students' brains magically empty after every holiday, snow day, or long weekend. Heck, they can even forget how to raise their hands overnight. Usually a quick review works just fine to get them back on track.

But what if you have a new student who will need more than just a quickie reminder? Here's a little-known trick that can help your new student learn your routines, save you time, and provide an in-depth review for the students in your class who need it the most.

The secret is to ask one of your challenging students to explain the classroom routines to the new student. Depending upon the situation and the students, you can pair up the students for the day or simply ask the challenging student to show the new student how to do one activity at a time. (Example: "Jason, would you please teach Juan about our schedule? Thanks, I appreciate it.")

I often find the challenging student provides a much more detailed explanation than I would! Sometimes the challenging student admits she has forgotten what to do. In that case, I pick another student to teach both of them. If your students try to get totally ridiculous and pretend they have all forgotten, then you have just boredom-proofed your whole-class in-depth review lesson.

Give it a try! Your new students will get the information they need, your challenging students will get to feel important, and you will be able to focus on other things, such as remembering where you put the projector remote.

WORRIED ABOUT BEING ABSENT?

DO YOU GO to school when you're sick because it's too much work to get ready for a sub? If you have to be gone for a meeting, do you worry what's happening in your absence? Will your room be a mess when you get back? Will you have to deal with discipline referrals, parent complaints, and student conflicts?

Although it is the substitute's job to maintain order while you are gone, there are a few things you can do to make it easier. And if the sub has a good day you won't have to waste time on damage control when you get back. Here are a few helpful hints:

1) Prepare your students ahead of time. Spend time teaching your students what you expect them to do when you are gone. Teach your expectations at the beginning of the year and review them (if possible) the day before you will be gone. If you can leave a written copy of your expectations for the sub so much the better. You can even request the sub rate your class on how well each expectation was followed (and/or have the students rate themselves) and reward your class accordingly when you return.

2) Make sure the students know their work will count even when you're gone. If you are a secondary teacher schedule a quiz, test, or graded assignment to be collected at the end of the period. If you're an elementary teacher provide individual work to reinforce what you've been doing in class. Avoid obvious throw-away activities such as word

searches, coloring, or assignments which have nothing to do with what you've been working on.

3) Think twice before leaving a video. In the first place, the room will be darkened, making it more difficult for the sub to see what's going on. In the second place, if there are technical issues with the video it will be very difficult for the sub to maintain control of the class and troubleshoot at the same time. In the third place, kids know adults use videos for babysitting, reinforcing the message that nothing counts when you are gone. If you do plan for the sub to show a video, require the students to take notes, take a quiz, or do a writing assignment about it.

4) Let the substitute teacher know what types of activities are acceptable for early finishers. Idle or bored students make trouble even for regular teachers. It's even worse for subs.

If you are sick or at a meeting you shouldn't have to worry what's happening in your class. Plan ahead so you will have peace of mind.

PUSH THE RESTART BUTTON BEFORE SPRING BREAK

I T WAS ALMOST Spring Break. As a first-year teacher I was fed up with the behavior issues in my classroom and I asked a more experienced teacher for advice. "Just grit your teeth and hold on until the end of the year," she said. "Next year you can make some positive changes but for this year it's too late."

This little gem of "wisdom" is totally untrue, and I sure wish I hadn't listened to it. It's basically just saying, "Give up! Let your students bully you, push you around, and run the show for the next four months. Then next year you can push the restart button and everything will be magically different."

Nothing can be further from the truth. This time of year is actually the perfect time to make some positive changes in your classroom, and if you've already given up hope for accomplishing anything academic with your students, what have you got to lose?

Let your students know you will be doing things differently after Break. You are going to teach them the new routines and procedures now so they will be prepared and know what to do. Then push that restart button and act like it's the first week of school. Teach classroom routines extensively. Show your students exactly how be successful in your new classroom environment and have them practice until they get it. You can even use some rewards to encourage them and possibly have a celebration of all they have learned on the Friday before Spring Break. Say how excited you are that everyone gets a new start the Monday after break and how you can't wait to see them and get started.

Then shut the door, lock it up, and go have a different kind of last-day-before-Spring-Break celebration with your colleagues and friends.

AFTER SPRING BREAK

D ID SPRING BREAK fly by? Were you thinking you would do your lesson plans later and you're now scrambling to figure out your activities?

Relax! Here's how to plan for your first day back after a long break.

Flip back in your plan book to the first week of school. Remember all those lessons about how to be a successful learner in your class? Repeat them! All those lessons about how to enter the room and get started on the warm-up assignment... how to ask the teacher for help... how to pack up at the end of class... how to head your paper and turn in your homework... and the list goes on and on, which is excellent news for you.

The first day back after an extended break is the perfect opportunity for both you and your students to get a do-over. If you have the time and energy I recommend a new seating arrangement. Meet your students at the door and greet them warmly as you let them in one at a time. Hand them a warm-up assignment, which can be an invitation to journal about what happened during the break, some questions or problems from your last unit to see what they still remember, an article or book to read, or a pre-test to see what they already know about an upcoming unit. Direct them to their new seats and ask them to quietly begin work on the warm-up assignment.

As soon as they are all in place, start going over all your procedures as if it's the first day of school again. If you want to make some changes, now is the perfect time to do it. It's like Groundhog Day in March! Both you and your students will get off to a better start, and it's easy-peasy planning for you.

CLOSING DOWN WITHOUT CHAOS

IT WAS THE last day of school and we were having a class party to celebrate. A parent was leading some party games that took forever. I knew it was getting late but I didn't know just how late until I looked up at the clock. We had only 30 minutes to clean up after the party and completely clean out all the students' desks and cubbies.

A wild scramble ensued with me barking out orders and the kids running around like little sugar-fueled tornadoes. The last minute of school arrived and then the last second. When the bell rang my students rushed headlong out the door with all sorts of paper and debris trailing behind them. I didn't even have a chance to say goodbye and the room was trashed.

Hours later when my teacher friends were busy toasting the end of the year at a party, I was desperately working to finish my end-of-the-year checklist.

It was horrible.

I am not a complete idiot, so why had I left everything to the last minute? Because a month before school ended, my principal directed us to make sure instruction continued right up to the last day of school. No shutting down early, she said. I interpreted this to mean the room had to be completely set up with all materials out until the last day of school. I have since learned this is not true. The room can be prepared for the end-of-the-year shutdown and learning can still occur. It's a balance. You can avoid the disaster I experienced by keeping some things in mind:

1) Your less socially able students need structure even more when a transition is nearing. You may be the most stable adult in your students' lives. Try to keep routines in place as long as you can to avoid those students freaking out, acting out, and testing the boundaries.

2) If possible, plan some sort of end-of-the-year project. One of my favorites is a keepsake book looking back over the major events of the school year. The students draw and write about each event in the book and take it home on the last day. Older students can create a portfolio of their best work and write a letter of introduction to the next year's teacher. Presentations, speeches, or demonstrations can also work well. Early project finishers can be recruited to organize books, pack boxes, and so on.

3) Collect textbooks and materials long before the last day of school and send things home gradually. You don't want to scramble at the last minute like I did, nor do you want the students lugging bags of stuff home on the last day.

4) Be strategic. Even though you collect many items ahead of time, your students still need activities to keep them engaged academically. One idea is to allow each student to choose a book from the class library to read during the last few days and take home to keep.

5) Make sure to leave time for some sort of a good-bye ritual on the last day of school. Students and teachers both need closure. Parties are good and so are book or tee-shirt signings. Just make sure to set firm boundaries and allow plenty of time for cleanup.

WHERE TO GET MORE HINTS

I HOPE YOU found these classroom management hints helpful. If so, you may want to become a free member of the Awesome Teacher Nation.

Members receive a classroom management hint (called the Monday Morning Sanity Boost) in their email inboxes each week.

To join, go to www.AwesomeTeacherNation.com, or email me at Katrina@AwesomeTeacherNation.

ABOUT THE AUTHOR

KATRINA AYRES HAS more than 20 years of experience teaching elementary and secondary students in both rural and urban settings.

She first discovered the importance of classroom management during her disastrous first teaching assignment in rural Hawaii, which she talks about in her first book, *All the Ways I Screwed Up My First Year of Teaching, and How You Can Avoid Doing It, Too* (available on Amazon.com.)

Through her own experiences, and with the help of mentors along the way, Katrina learned what really works in the classroom (and what doesn't.) She is now on a mission to teach other teachers what she has discovered using classroom management workshops and seminars, books, boot camps, coaching, and mentoring.

Katrina lives with her husband and her cat in a shiny glass building in Portland, Oregon.

Made in the USA
San Bernardino, CA
27 July 2018